Y0-CHY-713

YAMAHA BAND STUDENT

A BAND METHOD FOR GROUP OR INDIVIDUAL INSTRUCTION

by

Sandy Feldstein
John O'Reilly

Welcome to the world of MUSIC!

You now belong to a special group of musicians from all over the world whose lives are being enriched with music.

Membership in the YAMAHA BAND STUDENT course will provide you with a foundation for your future in music: as a composer, rock musician, teacher, conductor, symphony musician, or a listener enjoying the life-long benefits of music. It all starts here!

Your teacher's special skills, a fine instrument, your personal commitment and the YAMAHA BAND STUDENT is all it takes.

Welcome to the world of music, welcome to YOUR world!

Sandy Feldstein

John O'Reilly

Instrumentation

Flute
Oboe
Bassoon
Bb Clarinet
Eb Alto Clarinet
Bb Bass Clarinet
Eb Alto Saxophone
Bb Tenor Saxophone
Eb Baritone Saxophone
Bb Trumpet/Cornet
Horn in F
Horn in Eb
Trombone
Baritone T.C.
Baritone B.C.
Tuba
Percussion—S.D., B.D., Access.
Keyboard Percussion
Combined Percussion
Piano Accompaniment
Piano Accompaniment Cassette
Conductor's Score

Alfred

YAMAHA®
is a registered trademark of
Yamaha Corporation of America

1

TRUMPET FINGERING CHART

index finger   middle finger   ring finger

O = valve up
● = valve down

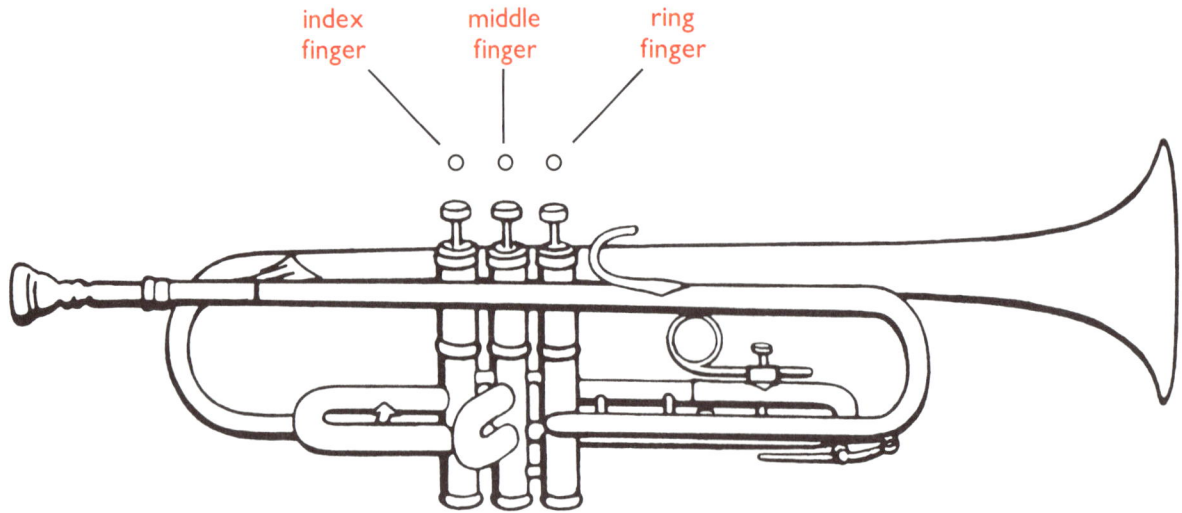

THE PARTS OF THE TRUMPET

mouthpiece receiver
mouthpipe
second valve
first valve
third valve
finger hook
bell section
mouthpiece
tuning slide
first valve slide
valve casings
third valve slide
tuning slide waterkey
second valve slide
third valve slide waterkey

STUDENT'S PRACTICE CHART

Name _____ To become a good musician you must practice every day. Find a convenient place where you can keep your instrument, book, music stand and any other practice equipment. Try to practice at the same time every day.

Week	MON	TUES	WED	THURS	FRI	SAT	SUN	Approval	Week	MON	TUES	WED	THURS	FRI	SAT	SUN	Approval
1									19								
2									20								
3									21								
4									22								
5									23								
6									24								
7									25								
8									26								
9									27								
10									28								
11									29								
12									30								
13									31								
14									32								
15									33								
16									34								
17									35								
18									36								

STAFF	TREBLE CLEF	BAR LINE	MEASURE	DOUBLE BAR

WHOLE NOTE	WHOLE REST	TIME SIGNATURE
o		$\frac{4}{4}$ = 4 beats to a measure
4 beats	4 beats of silence	$\frac{4}{4}$ = quarter note ♩ gets 1 beat

E	F	G

First Duet

Name the Notes—Then Play

6

QUARTER NOTE — 1 beat

QUARTER REST — 1 beat of silence

Hot Cross Buns

Go Tell Aunt Rhodie

e e d c c d d f e d c g g f e e e d c d e c

Merrily We Roll Along
Duet

e d c d e e e d d d e g g e d c d e e e e d d e d c

e d c d c c c d d d c e e e d c d c c c c d d e d c

Lightly Row

Go to next line

g e e f d d c d e f g g g g e e f d d c e g g e

d d d d d e f e e e e e f g g e e f d d c e g g c

A

REPEAT SIGNS

TEMPO MARKINGS
tell how slow or fast to play the music.
Moderato moderately
Allegro fast

1
f g a g a g a g a f g a g f

2
f g a g f d c a g f g a g f d e f c d e g f

Clap-and-Play Duet

Allegro

Clap

3

Jolly Old St. Nicholas
Duet

Moderato

4

5

aaaa ggg, ffff

ffff eee dddd f dddd cc f e d e c f

Just for Trumpets

$\mathbf{2}$ = 2 beats to a measure
$\mathbf{4}$ = quarter note gets 1 beat

TIE

connects 2 notes of same pitch

1

2

Two-Four March

Allegro

3

Good King Wenceslas
Duet

Moderato

4

fffg ffc dcde ff, fffg ffc dcde ff

5

c ce f dcdc cf c ce f dcdc cf

oinkoinks F   YukYuks FCCDCEF

Old MacDonald

Allegro

6

f f f c d d c a a g g f f c

f f f c d d c a a g g f f

Add the Barlines—Then Play

7

cdecggfedcc

f a f g c f

FULL BAND ARRANGEMENT

Jingle Bells

Arranged by SANDY FELDSTEIN
and JOHN O'REILLY

The Victors March

Arranged by SANDY FELDSTEIN
and JOHN O'REILLY

EIGHTH NOTES

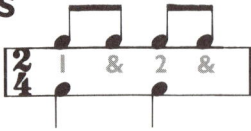

TEMPO

Andante
Moderately slow

1

1 & 2 & 3 & 4 &   1 & 2 & 3 &4&   1 & 2 & 3 &4&   1 & 2 & 3&4&   1 & 2 & 3 & 4 &   1 & 2 & 3&4&

2

1 & 2 &   1 & 2 &   1 & 2 &   1 & 2 &   1 & 2 &   1 & 2 &   1 & 2 &   1 & 2 &

Baa, Baa, Black Sheep

Andante

3

c c g g   a g a a g   f f e e   d d c   g g g f f f   e e e d

g g g f f f   e e e d   c c g g   a a a a g   f f e e   d d c

Up on the Housetop

Allegro

4

g g a g e   c e g   a a g e   d g g   g g a g e d

c e g   a g a g g e   d g c   f f a   g g e   d f f

e g g c e   g g a g e   f g a   g g a g e   d g c

Frère Jacques
Round   ②

Allegro

5

c d e c   c d e c   e f g   e f g

③   ④

g a g f e c   g a g f e c   c g c   c g c

Bb (B flat)

SLUR
connects notes of different pitch

1st and 2nd ENDING
2nd time

KEY SIGNATURE
This key signature tells you that all B's are played Bb.

1 Bb — Also played B flat

2

Yankee Doodle
3 Allegro
ffga fagc ffga fe ffga bagf ecde ff

Second Ending Blues
4 Moderate Rock
cegab agge
On repeat, skip to 2nd ending
cega bag gfeed cc

Good Night, Ladies
5 Andante — Duet

6

This Old Man
7 Allegro
geg geg agfe defef gecco cdefg gddf edc

Just for Trumpets

B

DOTTED HALF NOTE

3 beats

KEY SIGNATURE

This key signature tells you all notes are natural.

PICK-UP NOTES

(1 2 3)4   1   2   3   4

Not all music begins on beat 1. Notes before the first full measure are called pick-up notes.

1 B

2 1 2 3 4

Skip to My Lou

3 Allegro

Music in the Air

4 Andante

(1 2 3)4   1 2 3

Tom Dooley

Clap-and-Play Duet

Clap   Allegro

5

Add Barlines, Name the Notes—Then Play

6

$\dfrac{3}{4}$ = 3 beats to a measure = quarter note gets 1 beat	**ACCENT** >$ play the note louder	**DYNAMICS** tell how loud or soft to play. f (forte) loud p (piano) soft

1

Faith of Our Fathers

2 Andante

Pop Tune for Two
Duet

3 Allegro

4

Mexican Hat Dance

5 Moderato

Bb

STACCATO

play the note short

1 Bb | Also played B flat

2

Camptown Races

3 Allegro

There's a Hole in the Bucket
Duet

4 Andante

5

The Man on the Flying Trapeze

6 Moderato

Just for Trumpets

F♯ (F sharp)

KEY SIGNATURE

This key signature tells you that all F's are played F♯.

MULTIPLE MEASURE REST

Count 1 2 3 4 2 2 3 4

1 F♯ — Also played F sharp

2

Let's Row Again

3 Allegro

Erie Canal

4 Moderato

Rest Awhile

5 Moderato — Duet

6

16

FULL BAND ARRANGEMENT

Musette

J. S. BACH
Arranged by Sandy Feldstein
and John O'Reilly

Big Rock Candy Mountain

Arranged by SANDY FELDSTEIN
and JOHN O'REILLY

B

C

EIGHTH REST

$\frac{2}{4}$ 1 & 2 &

DIVISI

a divided part

DYNAMIC

mf

mezzo forte
medium loud

B   C

1 $\frac{3}{4}$

2 $\frac{4}{4}$

1 & 2 & 3 & 4 &   1&2&3&4&   1 & 2 & 3 & 4 &   1&2&3&4&   1 & 2 & 3 & 4 &   1&2&3&4&

C Scale and Chords

divisi

3 $\frac{4}{4}$

Polly Wolly Doodle

Moderato

4 $\frac{4}{4}$ *mf*

f   p   f

mf

Lovely Evening

Round

Andante

5 $\frac{3}{4}$ *mf*

②

③

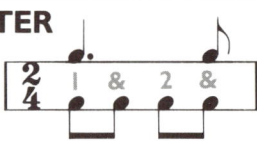

DOTTED QUARTER NOTE

1 1/2 beats

G Scale and Chords

divisi

All Through the Night

Andante   Duet

O Come All Ye Faithful

Allegro

Add Bar Lines, Name the Notes—Then Play

TEMPO

Vivo
Lively

C Scale Study

1

Jingle Bells

2 Allegro

The Dotted Quarter Clapping Band

3 Moderato

4

5

French Dance

6 Vivo

D.C. al Fine (Da Capo al Fine)

Go back to the beginning
and end at Fine.

G Scale Study

1

Alouette

2 Allegro · · · · · · · · · · · · *Fine*

mf *f* *p* *f* *p* *f* *D.C. al Fine*

Rock for Two

3 Moderate Rock — Duet

f

4

f

Just for Trumpets

CRESCENDO	DIMINUENDO
gradually get louder	gradually get softer

1

F Scale and Chords

2

Aura Lee

3

Surprise Symphony

HAYDN

4

We Wish You a Merry Christmas

Allegro

5

Number from Slowest (1) to Fastest (4)

6

___ Allegro   ___ Moderato   ___ Vivo   ___ Andante

22

LEGATO

Play as smoothly as possible.

F Scale Study

1

Chester

BILLINGS

2 Moderato

Molly Malone

3 Andante—Legato

Ode to Joy

BEETHOVEN

4 Moderato

eefg gfed ccde edd eefg gfed ccde dcc

dec defec defed cdgz eefg gfed ccde dcc

Just for Trumpets

D.S. al Fine (Dal Segno al Fine)

Go back to the sign 𝄋
and end at Fine.

Home on the Range

Andante

𝄋   *Fine*

D.S. al Fine

Smooth as Glass

Moderato   Duet

Give Me That Old Time Religion

Allegro   *Fine*

D.C. al Fine

FULL BAND ARRANGEMENT

Chorale and Allegro

SANDY FELDSTEIN
and JOHN O'REILLY

FERMATA

🖇 HOLD the note longer

Clap and Play Duet

1 & 2 & 3 & 4 & ...

C Technic Study
Duet

When the Saints Go Marching In
Allegro

Worried Man Blues
Moderato

Just for Trumpets

D	DYNAMIC	TEMPO
	mp	**Largo**
	mezzo piano—medium soft	very slow

1 (D)

2

Oh, Susanna

3 Allegro

mf fg accc cafg aagf

Largo from the New World Symphony

Largo — Duet — DVOŘÁK

4 *mp*

5 *mp*

Syncopated Rock

6 Moderate Rock — *f*

Bugle Call

7 Moderato — *mf*

Add Time Signatures—Then Clap the Rhythms

8

27

repeat the previous measure

1

G Technic Study
Duet

2

3

Volga Boat Song

Largo
4
mp

Happy Little Donkey
Round

Andante
5
mf

Travelin' to Arkansas

Allegro
6
mf

Fine
f

D.C. al Fine

Just for Trumpets

28

E

TIME SIGNATURE

𝄴 = common time
same as 4/4

E

1

Billy Boy

Allegro

2

Did You Ever See a Lassie?

Allegro

3

The Blue Bells of Scotland

Moderato   Duet

4

5

Number from Softest (1) to Loudest (4)

6   __ mf   __ p   __ mp   __ f

Minuet

BACH

Allegro
1
mf
1.
2.

Blue Tail Fly

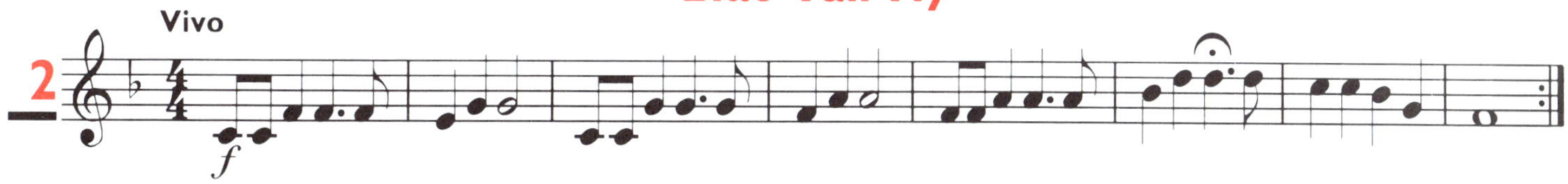
Vivo
2
f

Scarborough Fair

Moderato—Legato
3
mf

Dona Nobis Pacem

Round

Andante
4
mp
②
③

Auld Lang Syne

Moderato
5
mf

FULL BAND ARRANGEMENT

Rockin' On Home

SANDY FELDSTEIN
and JOHN O'REILLY

TRUMPET SOLO

Theme and Variation

Based on J. B. ARBAN

YAMAHA BAND STUDENT

CERTIFICATE
OF ACHIEVEMENT

YAMAHA BAND STUDENT

has successfully completed Book One of the
Yamaha Band Student and is promoted to Book Two.

_____
Band Director

_____
Date

_____
Authors